Revelation of Freedom

Lydia Rose Smith

NEW HARBOR PRESS

Rapid City, SD

Smith/New Harbor Press
1601 Mt, Rushmore Rd, Ste 3288
Rapid City, SD 57701
https://NewHarborPress.com

Ordering Information:
Quantity sales. Special discounts are available on quantity purchases by corporations, associations, and others. For details, contact the "Special Sales Department" at the address above.

Revelation of Freedom/Lydia Rose Smith. —1st ed.
ISBN 978-1-63357-475-5

Contents

Introduction

SINCE THE AGE OF four years old, God gave me a glimpse of the fruitful calling He has placed on my life. The strongest battles that we face are not of flesh and blood but of the spiritual realm. God has already paved the way for a beautiful path He has placed before you. The enemy will do whatever it takes to pull you off of that path. Through many trials and errors such as: experiencing death to life, generational curses, mental health battles, oppression and bondage, I finally discovered freedom. This is my testimony of how God delivered me through everything I used to view as a setback and used it to strengthen me and to inspire others with my testimony. From breaking off curses, experiencing miracles and radical healing, debunking all the lies of the enemy, and having a renewed mindset, the Lord fully restored me. I pray that this inspires you and that the Lord will reveal to you the full revelation of freedom. That you will be given every revelation on how to overcome any scheme of the enemy.

CHAPTER 1

Know Your Identity

THE BIGGEST THREAT A person can be to the devil is a person who knows their identity in Christ. Although there have been numerous times throughout my life I have forgotten my identity, God was so gracious to show me the influence I'm capable of at the ripe age of four years old. I have been blessed to have endured such an impactful experience that has forever changed my life, how I treat others, how I live on a day to day basis, and how I remember what life is truly about.

It was a hot summer day in Virginia, I remember standing in the garage as my mom opened the door and told me we'd be going shopping. She said she was going to take a nap before we left. I clearly didn't have a great concept of time at the age of four. I thought to myself: "Well, I'll just hop in the car and wait for her." So in my blue jean suit, with a bottle in my hand and about a quarter cup of milk remaining in the bottle, I hopped in the car, closed the door and waited. After a short amount of time I felt the heavy heat. So I tried opening the passenger side door and it wasn't opening. I proceeded to try to open other doors and nothing was opening. So I went on my way to make an even worse decision... buckle myself in my car seat. I could strap myself in but wasn't strong enough to unbuckle the large, safety-proof buckles.

Time felt slower than it had ever felt. I remember the feeling of that heavy, agonizing heat. I felt like I was in there for many hours but truthfully I don't know the time. There came a point when I figured I may be leaving the earth at a very young age. First, I thought of my family. I thought to myself, "They're going to miss me so much. They're always going to remember me as the little girl who never got to grow up." I was dreading the burden I would forever be bringing upon my family. Although I was in utter physical pain and worried for my family, it was the first time I felt such a strong super-natural peace come inside of me. A peace that made me know everything was going to turn out okay.

The peace numbed the pain but it didn't make it go away. I knew at a point I was reaching the end. I started to repeat one sentence over and over. "I'm gonna go home. I'm gonna go home. I'm gonna go home." Although I was at my physical home while I'm saying this, I referred to home as in the heavenly realm. I kept saying this until my vision blurred then my eyes shut as I got transported into another realm. I entered a tunnel that was long and felt like I was traveling in a time machine if those ever existed. Then all of the sudden it came to a stop and I remember everything went white. All I could see was myself with my short, blonde hair then across from me stood Jesus. He bent down with arms open wide and I ran up to Him and gave him the biggest hug. Then, God began speaking to me telepathically. He said that He has me here on this earth for a purpose, that He has big plans for me, and I'm going to change a lot of lives. He said it's not my time to go home yet. As I was hugging Jesus, I suddenly transported back into the tunnel. When it came to a stop again, my soul was back in my body, in the blazing hot car. Then the next moment, the car door opened and I got pulled out of the car. My body was gray from head to toe. The EMT showed up but I don't remember that part. Just everything else that happened in the vehicle. The following year, my siblings had made a remark about the incident and I followed up with this statement, "I died for a little bit that day." But I didn't discuss with anyone what happened because it felt too intimate to share the experience. But 15 years later, I began opening up about it. God pressed it on my heart to share this story since it plays a large role in my testimony.

Most people would say, "You're extremely lucky to still be alive." It's a miracle that I'm alive and I'm grateful for my life. But when you're in that situation, meeting Jesus on the other side, nothing else matters. Nothing in this world can compare to that feeling. You're never the same after experiencing the other side. I've never felt so free, so at peace, and so deeply loved.

My mom thinks I have no fear because of this experience. So many people are afraid of death. But boy, will that be an amazing day when the Lord takes me home for good.

This day has marked me. In the darkest moments of my life I've remembered this moment and it has truly saved me. At a young age God showed me that my life has purpose. It's been the reminder I've needed, that He has ordained me with an identity and nothing or no one can take that away. The vast majority of people are living a life having no sense of true identity. They have let the enemy snatch it away from them. I pray that God reveals to you the purpose He created you for and that you stand firm and confident in His calling on your life. I pray that He opens your eyes to see the truth of who you are and that He gives you the strength to rebuke the schemes of the enemy so that you may walk in fullness and freedom.

Romans 8:28 NIV And we know that in all things God works for the good of those who love him, who[a] have been called according to his purpose.

John 10:10 NIV The thief comes only to steal and kill and destroy; I have come that they may have life, and have it to the full.

It's heartbreaking to watch the youth in this generation being manipulated into believing they're someone they're not. From social pressure, false teachings in public schools, and the affirmation and attention from social media, mental health issues have skyrocketed within the past decade. Kids are being deceived into believing they are a pronoun that they're not, a problem that they're not, a mental disability that they're not. When parents fail to teach their kids the truth about who they are, the world will teach them that they're anything but what God created them to be. The dangers of social media is putting false, non-biblical identity on who someone is. *One of the most dangerous threats to the devil is a child of God who knows their identity in Christ.*

The devil tried to steal my identity from me when I was 15 and 16 years old. I fought battles I never thought I'd have to fight. Through dealing with perfectionism (OCD) and not reaching every unrealistic goal I set for myself, I was vulnerable enough to allow the spirit of depression to operate in my life and tell me lie after lie about who I was. I had already dealt with significant insecurities my whole life through my learning disabilities. Perfectionism felt like my escape from never feeling like I was enough; from never having a solid sense of worth or fulfillment. This also turned into disordered eating habits in order to control something in my life when it felt like nothing could go the way I planned. I felt as if I was walking around with chains weighing me down every day. Through expectations on social media, "friends" who only put me down, and mean comments I had received throughout my life, I had given those things power over my life and allowed them to dictate it. I eventually found myself so deep into believing the lies that the devil had spoken to me to the point where I believed the lie that it was time to take my life. I was deceived into believing that no one would really care or notice if I were gone. I was deceived into believing that it wouldn't make a difference for me to be in the world, that no one loved me, that I was worthless, that hell wouldn't feel much worse than what I was already living in. Through all of this there is one memory that stuck in the back of my mind and that's the time when I was four years old, dying from heat exhaustion when God said, "It's not your time yet. You're going to change a lot of lives." By the grace of God I am still here today, healed, free, and sharing my story, asking God to use it to help set people free from bondage and walk confidently in their God-given identity.

CHAPTER 2

Finding Freedom

I GREW UP IN a Christian, homeschooling family with 5 siblings. My older sister Evie, my three older brothers Liam, Wesley, and Jaden and a younger sister, Petra. We grew up in the church and went on missions trips to Ireland every summer. My parents were always very involved in the church. Although I seemed to "check all boxes" I was truly dealing with an identity crisis because I did not own my faith. I went to church because it was a chore. I didn't spend time with God outside of church. I didn't understand the meaning of a relationship with God. I was forced to attend youth group and hated it. I felt like I was hearing the same thing every time and many youth groups are unfortunately full of cliques which gave me another reason to not want to go.

At the age of 16, as I was battling an identity crisis, I was trying to decide if I wanted to live for the world or live for Jesus. I was riding a fine line in between which I believe is why the door opened for me to be battling mental illnesses. During this time God gave me my first prophetic dream. I was up in the clouds, alone and in a very confusing place. I was in between heaven and hell. The clouds were orange and yellow. It was so uncomfortable. I woke up and immediately knew it was God confronting me.

Revelation 3:15-16 NIV "I know your deeds, that you are neither cold nor hot. I wish you were either one or the other! So, because you are lukewarm—neither hot nor cold—I am about to spit you out of my mouth."

I was scared of giving my life fully over to Christ. I didn't want to let go of the idols I had in my life. I feared having to become a full time missionary and living a miserable life.

One day, my mom's friend was over and suggested I try the youth group at a small church in Purcellville, Virginia called The Victory House. Somehow I got convinced to go so I went to this youth group on a Tuesday night with my sister Petra and two of our friends. I had never seen anything like this before. It was a little scary. I knew the youth leader from the church both her and I used to attend years ago. She welcomed me with open arms. At the end of the night, leaders were walking around person-by-person praying for healing. Then to my surprise, people were getting healed! As someone who grew up in a church that not only rarely talked about the Holy Spirit but had never seen or believed these things actually happened, I had many questions. But something about the atmosphere made me think there was something there and I needed to come again. I felt something that I had never felt before. I felt the love of God when I went to that youth group. I felt a hunger and passion in the room for God. There was something there that I knew I was missing in my life. One night I heard my youth leader say something that suddenly made me realize what the answer was to all my problems. It's as if a lightswitch just went off immediately when I heard what she said and finally it all made sense. She said, "I opened up my Bible to spend time with the Lord and really wasn't feeling motivated to read it. But then I realized I was looking for answers for myself. So I shifted my focus while reading to learn about God and then I felt motivated to read it." When I heard this I suddenly understood that I kept trying to fix myself when all I needed to do was take the focus off of myself and fix my eyes on Jesus.

This was during my junior year of high school. It was my most challenging academic year, on top of playing sports, I was getting an average of 3-4 hours of sleep each night. But staying up late and giving myself over to Jesus each night was what I knew I needed to do. So I stayed up, worshiping the Lord, but most of all, I was acknowledging Him. There were a few songs I played on repeat. Those songs were "So Will I" by Hillsong United, "Oceans" by Hillsong United, and "Build My Life" by Pat Barret. I played "So Will I" over and over again, leaving every mental illness aside, just fixing my eyes on Jesus. The more I took the focus off myself and fixed my eyes on Him, the more He lifted chains off of me until He completely delivered me from my mental illnesses.

The Work Ethic Identity

There are many factors that go into why I attached onto unhealthy forms of identity. This topic is extremely underrated in society. It gets swept under the rug way too much due to politics and the coddle culture we're living in. Children are extremely vulnerable. It's easy to access dangerous data. It's easy to look at the lives of so many people and believe a lie from behind the screen of who someone is. These posts are highlights of someone's very unrealistic life. They highlight only the best areas of people's lives, insinuating a false sense of reality to the viewers who are subconsciously believing these lies and comparing their own lives to it.

As a teenager, I didn't think much of social media affecting my brain. I'm not naturally a jealous person so I didn't think it could have much of an effect on me. But then I realized, I used to put a lot of my identity into how I was perceived on social media because I didn't have a solid foundation of identity in who I was. There were many factors into why I dealt with mental health issues but I now believe that social media played about 50% of it. Everyone wants to be perceived well.

Vulnerability of a child

Children are vulnerable human beings, from the way they're treated as an infant, a toddler, a young child, a teenager, these are the most crucial years in the development of a human being. They don't understand how easily influenced they are until they become adults and then hopefully understand by looking back, why they made the life decisions they chose. As a young adult now, God has been opening my eyes up to see and understand the vulnerable moments in my life that opened up doors for the devil to torment me. Some instances were the result of an accumulation of events, others from a single sentence someone spoke over me.

*Proverbs 18:21 NIV "The **tongue** has **the power** of **life** and **death**, and those who love it will eat its fruit.* Word curses exist and this is something I wish I knew a long time ago.I want to be clear that if someone speaks over you in any negative way, it doesn't mean it has power over you. It only has power if you accept it. When you accept a curse someone speaks over you "You're weak, you're ugly, you don't work hard enough..." etc. Those are word curses. You can accept it or renounce it. Before I knew anything about having the power to renounce curses in the name of Jesus, I accepted those curses, therefore I came into agreement with the devil's plan. The sole purpose of that plan was to torment my life. By accepting and believing lies spoken over me, I unknowingly gave the devil permission to oppress me through the spirit of depression, an eating disorder, anxiety, and OCD. I always thought these mental issues were a result of me being a failure. And for those who say that these things can't be 100% reversible, that is a lie from the pit of hell and I'm living proof that God can heal anyone 100%.

CHAPTER 3

Fully Devoted

I WAS TRULY SCARED that if I devoted my life over to Christ, I would be miserable because I couldn't follow my dreams. I thought that in order to be fully devoted I would have to give up everything I loved and move to a third world country to become a missionary. When I was 16, my youth pastor gave a message, giving some of the best advice I had ever heard. She said, "When you are following Jesus, He won't allow you to be miserable, He's too good of a Father for that." Society can paint such a false image of the Father that God is. He's often falsely framed as only disciplinary rather than the loving, and forgiving Father that He is. I had never opened up my life to experience the fullness of God's love. The thought of God truly wanting me to be happy is not something

I took into consideration at the time. Turned out that the things I struggled to give up, I no longer have any desire for to this day. I have found that the closer I get to God, the more I fall in love with Him. And the more I fall in love with Him, the less I care about anything in this world. Being a Christian is hard. But not being a Christian can be a lot harder. As a Christian you have to make a lot of sacrifices, you endure suffering and much rejection. You experience persecution and you are called to a life of selflessness. But those sacrifices can't even compare to what you receive in return. There is nothing more valuable than a relationship with Jesus. You will experience the kind of peace, joy, and fulfillment that the world could never give you. My hope is that by the end of this book, you will understand the beauty and value of having Jesus as the foundation in your life.

Devotion to the Lord is the most important, beautiful decision a person can make. I got baptized at 7 years of age. But I truly gave myself over to Jesus as a desperate teenager seeking for help. I remember at 17 during the 2020 Covid pandemic, I felt a stirring in my heart. I felt a spark that would eventually turn into a blazing fire for the Lord. I wanted to be fully devoted.

Fully devoting your life to Jesus means giving up the desires of your flesh. It means cutting out the sin in your life. It means pleasing God over pleasing man. Devotion doesn't look perfect but Jesus isn't expecting perfection from you. He's expecting an open heart. The Lord calls us to yield to Him, to give our "I will" in whatever He calls us to do.

Proverbs 3:5-6 NIV

> Trust in the LORD with all your heart, and lean not on your own understanding; in all your ways acknowledge Him, and He will make your paths straight.

Matthew 6:5-6 NIV

> "And when you pray, do not be like the hypocrites, for they love to pray standing in the synagogues and on the street corners to be seen by others. Truly I tell you, they have received their reward in full. But when you pray, go into your room, close the door and pray to your Father, who is unseen. Then your Father, who sees what is done in secret, will reward you."

God knows the posture of your heart. He sees through every area of your heart. There have been many times in my life I thought that I gave something over to the Lord because I gave it to Him verbally, but not in my heart. You know your heart better than other people and God knows your heart in every aspect of your life.

The presence of Jesus is an honor - not a chore.

I used to be hesitant about going all-in with God because I didn't want to give up the things that brought me joy. Even though those weren't bad things, I had made an idol out of them because I put them before God.

I used to never open my Bible on my own. The few times that I would open it up, it felt like a chore. I didn't understand what having "quiet time" with the Lord meant - I didn't understand the importance of it, how to go about it, or how to get anything out of it. But that was the problem. From my understanding, it was about receiving answers for my questions. When we're making a relationship self-centered, it's not about the love of the other person. The same goes for our relationship with Jesus. Once I stopped focusing on having all of my questions answered and problems fixed, everything changed.

Just like any relationship, it's not going to be perfect and we won't have all the answers.

Your Praise Should Be Unconditional

If God's love for us is unconditional, why should our praise be conditional? I have found myself falling into a pattern of praising the Lord the most when I'm broken, tired, or fighting for my life. Then when things are going well, I've taken a step back from praise, excited and distracted by the blessings God has given to me, forgetting to keep Him at the throne of my heart. Maybe the Lord will bless those who praise Him through the highs and lows even more. But if He does, that's not the point. The point is running into the arms of the Father through the heartaches, the setbacks, through the wins, and through the breakthroughs. If God loves me just the same through my highs and lows, am I reflecting my love, praise, and devotion to Him unconditionally or only when it's convenient? It requires maturity, a humble heart, and a genuine love for the Lord to be resilient and unwavering in our praise.

Your praise is a weapon.

> God's high and holy praises fill their mouths, for their shouted praises are their weapons of war! These warring weapons will bring vengeance on the nations and every resistant power—to bind kings

with chains and rulers with iron shackles.

Praise-filled warriors will enforce the judgment decreed against their enemies.

This is the honor he gives to all his godly lovers.

Hallelujah! Praise the Lord!

Psalms 149:6-9 TPT

CHAPTER 4

The Process of Refinement

THE MORE INTENTIONAL YOU are in your relationship with Jesus, the more He will refine your character.

Every believer walks through seasons of refinement. These seasons are pivotal for preparing you for the next season.

How do you know if you're in a refinement season? First of all, the more we grow in the Lord, the more He refines our character in our walk with Him. But there's a difference between God working on an area in your life and walking through a season of refinement. Typically, a season of refinement is a very difficult process.

And if you don't learn your lesson the first time through, God might not let you exit it until you have changed.

You're Never Alone

Reaching your breaking point

The times throughout my life I have come closest to God were in the darkest, hardest, most lonely times. Imagine having been homeschooled (very sheltered) your whole life. You lived on a farm, having very few friends or social life. Then an opportunity came up out of the blew that required moving across the country to a place you had no connections, living by yourself, leaving your beloved pet behind, all to risk it for a dream where there's no guarantee. That's exactly what I did at 20 years old. It was the scariest, hardest, most frustrating year of my life.

My biggest year of refinement was the year I moved out on my own for the first time. Two years ago, I began traveling across the country to follow my dreams. It was my first time moving out, my first time living on my own, and my first time living apart from my family at 20 years old.

I left my home in Virginia at about 4:00 am. My dog, Pippa, could sense that I was leaving and jumped in the car, waiting for me. Leaving her behind was heartbreaking but I chose growth over comfort. One of my best friends helped me with the first leg of the trip to Nashville and my brother (bless his heart) drove with me for the rest of the 40 hour road trip to Southern California. My parents flew in for a few days and helped me unpack. I will never forget the feeling after dropping my brother and parents off at the airport. My heart sank, I cried a little, and everything just hit me at once. It was me versus the world for the first time and that was a scary, exciting new thing.

April 2023 - May of 2024 was the duration of time I spent living in California. It was the loneliest year of my life and one of the hardest. I moved out on a promise that did not get delivered. I uprooted my entire life based on a promised opportunity. I lived in a 400sq ft studio apartment, right by a church building. It was a rather sketchy area. The first week I moved in, someone backed into my car parked in the parking lot. The second week, my studio became infested with cockroaches (my biggest fear) and the third week, I had many major unexpected expenses. The fourth week, I learned that the promises that were made to me were not going to be delivered which defeated my whole purpose of moving out there. Everything going on felt like a slap in the face. The gym I moved to train as a full time athlete ended up being a toxic environment. Ninety percent of the time I got excluded from group activities, glared at or yelled at for simply being in the same space.

There were a few friendly faces but when the majority of people make you feel unwelcomed, it sets you up for imposter syndrome, especially as someone who is young and giving the dream a shot. A month in, I got a connection for a job offer as a barista at a coffee shop. I worked there for about two months. I was transparent with them from the start and let them know that due to my learning disabilities, it takes me a while to learn new things. The hiring manager rarely came in. For whatever reason, the supervisor seemed to hold something against me. She asked the manager to fire me for not having learned things fast enough. I spent hours each day during non-work hours trying to memorize forty different recipes but that didn't cut it. Having come in and being fired was truly one of my biggest nightmares as someone who tries their best even when no one notices it. I'll never forget that day I got laid off. I called my mom in tears. I couldn't believe that that happened to me. I've always put so much of my identity in working as hard as I could in whatever I do and this crushed me.

I spoke with some people and soon got a job at a fancy hotel. I started off organizing the mini bar in each hotel room, then after a couple weeks of that I got an offer to switch to valet at this hotel so I ended up doing valet for almost a year. I trained at the gym 5-6 hours a day then valeted in the evening/night for 5-6 hours, six days a week. I had almost no free time and I didn't make any friends until the thirteenth month I lived there. I missed my friends and family. I missed my dog. I had many mental breakdowns in my car and in my studio.

I cried out to God for help because I couldn't live like this much longer. What were occasional breakdowns turned into an everyday breakdown. I felt a type of loneliness that I never felt before. I experienced a level of rejection I had never experienced before. But something in me knew since the beginning of the move, that God brought me there for a much greater purpose than becoming a full time CrossFit athlete. I just couldn't figure it out. But in this difficult season, God was refining my character. Here are the top 6 lessons I learned during this time:

1. Put all trust in God. There will be lots of tears no one (but God) will ever see and you're going to learn how to independently navigate your emotions. This year brought me closer to God than I had ever been because He's all I had to hold onto, all I had to trust, and He never failed me no matter how hard things got.

2. Learning to hear God's voice. I felt as if I was being pulled in multiple directions. People will

give you advice. Some people will give you good advice, some people will give you terrible advice. If you don't want the life they have, take what they give you with a grain of salt. But most importantly, value what God is telling your heart because that's way more important than listening to anyone else's opinion.

3. When you move out, you will know who your real friends are. It will automatically remove people from your life that need to be removed and will reveal who cares about you deeply. My closest friends got even closer when I moved, despite being on the opposite side of the country. I don't know how I would've done it without them.

4. Have self respect. When you move, you learn how necessary boundaries are. You will quickly learn that a large majority of the world will want to take advantage of you, leading you to realize you have to know your worth.

5. Have grace for yourself. When you move out, you will have bills you never even thought about and a lot more stress on your plate. You want to give all you've got. But sometimes giving your everything may look different than you expected. Sometimes giving your everything is simply showing up.

6. Your environment matters more than you think. If it's robbing you of your peace or joy or you feel like you can't be yourself, it's time to move. Don't let your current environment take a toll on your mental health.

Living on my own, having moved cross-country twice to two different areas within two years, I didn't know anyone and yes, it was hard. But was it worth it? Would I have been better off staying at home from an emotional toll standpoint? As an athlete, maybe. As a human being, absolutely not - I wouldn't know how to navigate the world. If I hadn't moved, I wouldn't have developed the self respect I needed. I wouldn't have learned to put 100% trust in God. I wouldn't have learned the value in community and relationships. So yes, I do recommend taking the leap of faith and seeing what happens.

You're going to reach your threshold.
Gold gets refined through fire. Fire is necessary in testing and removing any impurities. It has to burn. It has to bring up every flaw to the surface in order to be made pure. God takes us through a similar process while refining us. He will expose every impurity. He will test your threshold. He will allow you to walk through fire, allowing you the opportunity to trust Him.

My year living in California was a year of refinement. Although it was the most challenging time of my life, I ended up drawing closer to God than I had ever been. I gained so much appreciation for my family and friends that I dearly missed from across the country. I cried many tears but found myself on my knees crying out to God more than I had ever done. I found myself in situations where my two choices were giving up or having faith. God never failed me. He increased my faith immensely in this season and never allowed me to enter a situation I could get burned from without healing.

Breakthrough starts with surrender

I recently had a conversation with a friend who asked, "How do you surrender everything to God?" The truth is that it takes faith. Every time I've held on so close to something, particularly idols in my life, God let me reach my breaking point where holding onto it wasn't serving me any purpose. There was no way through other than a miracle and I had to lay that dream down before the Lord, not just with my words, but with my whole heart. Every time I fully surrendered that dream or situation over to God, He truly parted the waters and blessed me in more ways than I ever could have imagined.

CHAPTER 5

Spiritual Warfare/ Spiritual Gifts

As a Christian it's inevitable that you will face spiritual warfare. Spiritual warfare is the battle between God's kingdom and Satan's kingdom. When you are doing anything to benefit the kingdom of God, there's a high chance you will face many obstacles. The devil can hinder you but he can't stop you.

During the mission trips my family took every summer and building up to them, all of us faced immense spiritual warfare. We had several incidents where a beloved animal almost died while we were away, someone would come down with an unknown sickness leading to hospital visits, crazy logistical issues you just can't explain, and so much more. I'll never forget the moment in summer of 2016 when my mom received a phone call from the pet sitter about my new horse who meant the world to me. "I went to bring Sahara in from the field today and she could hardly move her legs. I have the vet out here and we believe she broke her femur." I cried myself to sleep that night. The next day, we got news that things were getting worse. I remember my mom telling me this in the car. She said, "It's looking like Sahara will have to be put down within the next few days." How could this happen? I finally got my dream horse. My parents spent so much money on her. I haven't even had her for a year yet. I remember thinking, "Something about this just doesn't quite feel real." To this day, I don't know how to best describe the way I felt. This was the second time in my life that I experienced anything like this. I was devastated on the outside. I cried constantly and just wanted to be home. But on the inside, there was this warm blanket around me, telling me that everything was going to be okay. It was as if my soul knew everything was going to be okay but my flesh had a hard time accepting it. That was the Holy Spirit.

I remember my parents discussing whether or not me and my mom should go home so that I could say my goodbyes. It felt like it made sense, but it also didn't feel right. We waited another day and got word that she was making some small progress. So we decided to stay in Ireland and finish the mission trip. When we got home she was 90% of the way there and within a few days she was 100% healed. Taking our eyes off of the prize is exactly what the devil wanted. Going home from the trip that's intended to spread the gospel is exactly what the devil wanted to happen. This is why the enemy uses spiritual warfare on followers of Jesus. To distract them from the mission, to discourage them and try to make them give up, to find their weak spots, to test if they're willing to fold at their breaking point.

When I made the decision to write this book, I opened up my laptop to start, and as soon as I was about to start, a bunch of lines popped up and I couldn't see the screen. So I actually began this book on my iPhone. My laptop having issues all of the sudden just didn't seem like a coincidence, it was confirmation. A couple months later, the issue resolved on its own.

The devil will attack your spiritual gifts

One of my spiritual gifts from the Lord is prophecy, specifically through dreams. I go through phases of my life where I receive a revelation through a dream from time to time. I go through long periods of not receiving any dreams and then I go through phases of receiving spiritual dreams just about every night for a long period of time. Usually when this happens, something major in my life is about to happen or change.

Let me be clear, not every dream is spiritual and not every spiritual dream is from God. Most of the time I can discern whether or not a dream is spiritual and whether or not it's from God. But because the devil knows that dreams are one of the major ways the Lord speaks to me, he often tries to attack me through my dreams.

Most of the time when I receive a dream then wake up, I write it down and ask God for the revelation. Sometimes I know what He was speaking to me immediately and sometimes it takes a while before God will reveal it to me. That's very common with prophecy. I typically don't write down dreams that were attacks because I have no reason to come into agreement with anything the devil attempts to attack me with. However, if I'm noticing a specific pattern in nightmares, I'll jot it down to put the pieces together to make sure I have everything in check in my life. As true followers of Christ, we receive conviction from the Lord about sin that will pull us away from Him. I have found that the stronger my relationship grows with the Lord, the more I get convicted of worldly things. There are very few movies or television shows that I will watch and I typically don't watch anything over a PG-13 rating. TV has been something that the Lord has strongly convicted me about. I have found that if I have even a subtle conviction about something I'm watching and I ignore it, there's a 99% chance I have opened up a door spiritually that leads to horrific nightmares and I will come to the Lord for repentance from it. I don't address this for having a legalistic or fear-based approach to anything. But I address this because it's important to listen to the Holy Spirit when He's speaking to you and realize that as a follower of Christ we must prioritize guarding our hearts, mouths, and ears from anything that may come between us and Christ. What you engage in and who you engage with, impacts your relationship with God.

Proverbs 4:23 NIV Above all else, guard your heart, for everything you do flows from it.

Spiritual Gifts

Every person on this planet has been given spiritual gifts. People who are in a relationship with Jesus have likely recognized or soon will know what some of those spiritual gifts are. There are so many people who die not ever knowing that they had a spiritual gift. For non-believers they can be falsely pinned as having a mental disorder. For instance, bipolar disorder may in fact be the spiritual gift of discernment. But if someone with this diagnosis is not walking in one with the Holy Spirit, they may never know they have this gift. I personally believe that most people have been given the gift of discernment whether it's strong or not. Think about the times throughout your life when you had a 'gut feeling' about something. Did your literal gut tell you that something was happening? I believe that it's a gift. Every single person who follows Jesus has the responsibility to carry that gift with them at all times and use it wisely. The gift of discernment gives believers the sense to recognize traps that the enemy has set up. Sometimes this gift will appear as a 'gut feeling' in your stomach and you don't know why but it's important to not ignore it. It could be a strong warning to help turn you away from danger, a sign to pray off attacks, and oftentimes it's given to determine truth from falsehood. I've noticed that the strongest believers I know all have very strong discernment. Your level of discernment is a reflection of your walk with Jesus.

The more you spend time with Jesus the more your senses sharpen. Faith is like a muscle. The harder the pressure gets tested under, the stronger it grows. Gold has to undergo extreme pressure in the process of being purified. I remember once hearing a pastor say, "I have never grown in an easy season."

Take the time to ask God to open your eyes to what He's showing you in the season you're in. You might get an immediate answer. You might not. Sometimes the answer is right in front of your face. Sometimes the answer is something you'll only know on the other side. Maybe you're wondering where God is in this season. But have you ever heard someone yell who's standing right next to you?

CHAPTER 6

Forgiveness is the Root/ Deliverance

WHEN YOU ARE HOLDING onto unforgiveness it will hinder you.

I have experienced an immense amount of pain through past relationships in my life. So much pain that made me believe I never wanted to be in a relationship. I got bullied a lot as a kid for having a learning disability. I had little to no confidence because of my disability and never stood up for myself.

I remember when I had recently moved to Georgia and was listening to a sermon at church on the topic of forgiveness. Later that night I was thinking how powerful of a sermon it was but thought, "That's not something I struggle with." Then I heard, "Oh yes, you do." In that moment the Lord convicted me of a deep rooted issue I wasn't even aware of.

Take a second to think about any past painful memories when you were hurt by someone and ask yourself these questions. Do these memories pop up frequently? How do you feel towards that person when they pop up and do you remember how painful it was? Do you wish them well? Do you talk about the incident frequently? Do you gossip about them? Do you just say that you forgive them? Do you actually forgive them?

There's a difference between saying "Sorry God" or "I forgive them", verses meaning what you're saying in your heart. Remember that God knows your motives. I had to learn how to forgive. Learning to forgive is often a process that takes time. Most spiritual oppressions stem from unforgiveness. In a deliverance, the first step should be walking through every area of your life where there is any unforgiveness and truly forgiving those people.

Spiritual deliverance is the act of being freed or rescued from negative spiritual influences, oppression, or bondage, such as demons, by a divine power, through Jesus Christ.

Many people have run to modern age demonic practices such as; tarot card readings, astrology, crystals, or psychics to try to free themselves from the bondage they're in while unknowingly opening up more doors for demons to come in and torment their lives even more. The only way that we can walk in full freedom is to surrender our lives to Jesus, the one who defeated all darkness on the cross. For He holds all power and authority.

People believe when they seek these practices that they are communicating with their relatives who have passed away or they feel temporary validation by being told by a psychic about details of their life that no one knew about but themselves. The truth is that fortune telling is channelled through demons who as we know from the Bible, only come to steal, kill, and destroy. It's supposed to sound enticing and validate you in the moment. Demons are real and they study everyone. They've been watching you your whole life and they know your weak spots more than you do.

Acts 2:21 NIV And everyone who calls on the name of the Lord will be saved.

If you've given your life over to Jesus then you have the Holy Spirit dwelling in you which means there cannot be demons dwelling in you. However, they can oppress you. I had been oppressed for most of my life by the spirit of rejection. This was a generational curse on a line of the women in my family and God brought me through the fire to break that curse off of my life.

Here is my deliverance story:

Since moving to Georgia, God has healed and restored me in wounded areas I didn't even realize needed healing. I've never felt so free in my life as I do now and I know I haven't fully reached restoration in every single area of my life yet. The exact amount of time I spent living in Southern Ca (13 months) is the exact amount of time it has taken me to mentally, emotionally and physically heal from that year. I am now free from all of the oppression I was under and everything the devil was shooting at me to hinder me from what the Lord has in store for me. After 6 months of living in Georgia, I joined a small group of believers from the gym and ended up meeting the leader of the group for a deliverance session. It's important to seek a strong, trustworthy person who closely follows the Lord and knows how to guide you through a deliverance. These ought to be guided appropriately and executed with intention, as the purpose is to break curses (demonic strongholds) off of your life. I told her my whole life story, the good, the bad, the ugly. Before moving on to any difference where we pray and talk to God, one of the first things that needs to happen is forgiving everyone who you've held onto any unforgiveness from. It was a very powerful session and we rebuked a lot of things in the name of Jesus. Once we got to the deliverance part and rebuked rejection off of my life, it physically manifested as it was leaving my body. I felt it come up through my throat first then broke into a sweat and started hyperventilating as it left.

But what was interesting is that even though a lot of things were broken off of me that day, other areas of my life took time. The next day, I decided to go through every person I could think of who hurt me and forgive them not just in my heart but out loud. The more I kept mentioning names, the more they kept popping up. After putting constant repentance as a priority in my life, I have never felt so free.

Matthew 3:8 NIV Produce fruit in keeping with repentance.

Forgiveness does not come to us naturally. God calls us to live in a constant state of repentance. There are 3 essential steps to get to this state. 1: Awareness. 2: Conviction. 3: Practice.

The closer you get to God, the more you will be convicted of the things of the world. He renews the minds of those who draw near to him. John 6:35 says, "I am the **bread of life**; whoever comes to me shall not hunger, **and whoever believes in me shall never thirst.**"

CHAPTER 7

Walking by Faith

DEFINITION OF FAITH: COMPLETE trust or confidence in God

It took my whole life until now to realize that I have been so attacked through thoughts, word curses, and unfaithful friends throughout my life, because the enemy knows my strongest gift - the gift of faith. He will do anything to make me crumble. But no matter how many arrows he shoots at me to make me lose my confidence and complete trust in the Lord, God always takes what the enemy meant for evil and turns it to good. I always come out stronger; no matter how hard my faith has been tested. God has never let me down.

Have you ever heard of the phrase, "You become your five closest friends?" Who you spend time with, matters. I've met people who were walking on solid ground until they got close with the wrong people. Faith is like a muscle. The more you exercise it, the stronger it gets. In the Bible (Luke 5) Jesus healed a paralyzed man because of His friends' faith. Who you spend time around matters. God gave me the gift of faith. That gift began blossoming when a friend of faith came into my life.

I was eighteen at the time. It was my last year of high school. My horse, Sahara, had recently and unexpectedly passed away. I had no friends and was grieving the loss of her. I wasn't sure if I would ever recover from it. I met for coffee with my amazing youth leader at the time. She broke the news to me that God called her and her husband to move to South Africa to become full time missionaries. We then walked next door to the church building before youth group was going to start that night. We were outside on the stairs and she asked to pray over me. Without having discussed relationships, she said, "I really feel like God is asking me to pray for a best friend in your life." After youth was over that night, I ended up in a deep conversation with a girl I had been acquaintances with for a while. We had no idea until that night, how parallel, yet opposite, our lives were in many ways. That night, I knew God answered that prayer immediately. Maddie and I quickly became close friends. After youth group, she would tell me amazing stories of faith. She talked about faith a lot, how she worked on growing it and how she aspired to have a stronger level of faith in her life. She woke me up to the reality of what living out radical faith looks like.

Breaking soul ties

Every time I had a conversation with Maddie, God was clearly moving in my life. On Thanksgiving in 2022, Maddie came to my house at the end of the day to hang out. As we were chatting in my room, I brought something up that I had been pressing on my heart. My bedroom was covered with well over 700 ribbons and trophies from all the horse shows I had attended throughout my entire life. I had a massive picture frame with a beautiful photo of Sahara in it that I had hid in my closet because I couldn't stand to look at it when she passed away. I said to Maddie, "For some reason something feels off about all of these ribbons." She said, "You know, I've never mentioned anything, but something about it has always made me feel off too." So I said, "Well, do you want to help me take them all down?" So we pulled out some trash bags and began stripping the walls. There was a moment where she said to pause and that God was speaking. She said, "The devil is trying to hinder you from moving forward by reminding you of your past every morning when you wake up and see these ribbons." So many things suddenly clicked at that moment. I said, "Every trophy, every ribbon, or anything with Sahara on it, I want it gone." We then got to the closet where the picture frame of Sahara was sitting. Maddie said, "Wait, you had a soul tie with her!"

"I had a what?" I said. That was the first time I had heard of that term. A soul tie is *a deep, often spiritual or emotional connection between two people, whether in romantic, familial, or platonic relationships, that goes beyond a typical friendship or partnership.* A soul tie can form between you and another being, it's not always another person.

After we cleaned out my room, it felt free. It felt like a true breath of fresh air for the first time. Maddie picked up a rock I had sitting on my dresser. That rock had been given to me at a youth group camp a couple years prior. The youth pastor prayed over all of these rocks for each student and asked for a word for them and painted it on the back. I never knew what it meant but I knew that God was going to reveal the meaning of it one day. The word on the rock was 'Forward.' Since that night, I felt free. I felt like a boulder had been lifted off my back, but there were still some small rocks to clean up.

Having faith means putting your full trust in God, despite what sounds logical. God overrules logic. There are tests of faith the Lord has put me through where on paper, I knew what made the most sense, but in my heart, God gave me discernment and told me to trust Him over logic. Here's one example:

In December of 2024, I went home for a month to travel with my parents to compete in Europe then stay with them until Christmas. I drove with my dog, Pippa, from Georgia to Virginia. At this point, I had just finished a 5 month work contract and had no idea what God had in store for me. It was a pretty stressful trip considering I was not going to be working until I hopefully would find a job after Christmas when I went home. When I drove to Virginia with Pip, I packed all of her belongings thinking there was an 80% chance I would be leaving her with my parents who were open to taking her in. How can I make enough money finding a full time job and owning a dog? I just couldn't leave her home all day. Every time the thought crossed my mind of leaving her in Virginia,, it broke my heart. The night before driving back to Georgia, I for sure thought Pippa wouldn't be coming with me. But over the course of several hours, I could hear God telling me to take her and trust that He had a plan. The morning before leaving, I said to my parents, "God is testing my faith right now; I'm going to take her with me." The very next day I arrived back in

Georgia, I met with a couple looking for a nanny and they agreed to let me bring Pippa to work. It has been a huge blessing!

Just because there's an open door doesn't mean you should walk through it. Take the time to pray about it. Does it give you peace? Do you have questions or confusion about it?

Another example of exercising faith:

When I lived in California working as a valet, one night a woman who was an overnight guest turned her raggedy car over to us. As soon as she parked it in the front driveway, we tried turning on the vehicle to move it to one of the lots but it wasn't turning on. Typically if it has any juice you will hear at least a subtle clicking sound but we got nothing. This car was completely dead. So there was a plan in place to have the vehicle towed. A couple hours later, I heard this soft voice in my head, "Go pray over it." So I listened. My co-workers were not present at this time but I took the key, hopped in the car, and asked that God would fix it. After I prayed I inserted the key, turned it, and the car turned on. I proceeded to park it in one of the lots then returned to the valet stand where my co-workers were standing. A few minutes later, they exclaimed, "Wait! Where is the car?!"

I said, "I parked it."

"How in the world did you do that? How is that possible?" they asked. I told them that I said a prayer then it worked.

That day, some seeds were planted. When you exercise faith, it will plant seeds in the people around you. Listen and be obedient when God is pressing something on your heart and watch what happens.

I've seen many miracles in my life. I believe that this miracle I'm about to tell was given to me as a reminder to 1: have faith even in the little things, and 2: God cares about the minor areas of our lives too.

For Christmas one year, I was given a used espresso machine off of Facebook marketplace. I was so excited about it, but it only lasted about 3 months before the machine broke. It stopped pouring not just espresso but any form of liquid out of it. None of the buttons worked, and when I plugged it in, steam came out of every crevasse. It was so disappointing. But one day, I got an itch to take a video of the broken machine because I had a feeling that God was going to fix it. Suddenly, I heard in my mind, "Pray over it." So I did without a question. I prayed over my espresso machine. Then pulled out my camera for what I believed was a miracle I was about to witness. I plugged it in, turned it on, pressed the bottom, and it made coffee. No steam came out of any crevice, it was

working, 100% fixed after being completely bust-
ed right before I prayed over it. I still have those
videos of before and after and I still use that machine to this day (4 years later).

Have childlike faith

Truly I tell you, unless you change and become like little children, you will never enter the
kingdom of heaven". Matthew 18:3 NIV

I didn't know how fulfilled I could feel from
a job until I became a nanny. It's taught me more
than any other job has. It's fulfilled that feminine
side of me that God created - the gift of to serve
others. It brings me down to reality, teaches me to
fully embrace every moment, and find joy in the
little things. It reminds me how life isn't supposed
to be too serious. It heals childhood wounds in
me and makes me feel like a child again - not in
an immature way but in the sense of having more
joy. It makes me excited to become a mom one
day. A job that I questioned if I ever wanted, for
most of my life.

One day while at work, I was stacking up
some blocks with a two year old. We were half
playing Jenga, then at one point I decided, "You
know what... we're playing this game." I've always
been a competitive person. I tend to do well with
games because I'm generally pretty good at fig-
uring out someone's thought pattern, knowing

their next move, then using it to my advantage. However, apparently that tactic goes out the window when you're playing with a toddler. At one point, he ended up beating me... genuinely. I sat there in awe. I could not believe that a toddler just beat me at Jenga. Then the following day, he beat me again. Then it struck me - he wasn't thinking about his next move, or if he was, he wasn't thinking about it very hard. So I wasn't able to read where he was going. It reminded me that this very much applies to our own lives. It's our instinct to take control over everything in our lives - to hold on tightly to our own will, being anxious about things we're holding on to so tightly. We try to control areas of our lives that we have no business controlling. But trying to take control of our own will can do us more harm than good. God tells us to let go of our own will and He will never lead us astray. *Proverbs 3:5-6 (NIV):*

> *"Trust in the LORD with all your heart and lean not on your own understanding; in all your ways submit to him, and he will make your paths straight."*

The definition of faith is complete trust or confidence in the Lord. It was such an eye opening moment the day I realized that the reason why my mind has been attacked by arrows of doubt so much throughout my life is because the Lord gave me the gift of faith.

It's okay if you have doubts. Faith wouldn't be required without doubt. However, doubt counters faith. So we're called to be courageous, to seek faith in the midst of doubts.

I love working with children because they have so much hope. They have this natural tendency to have faith in what they have not yet seen. Then through trials and trauma, as children transform into adulthood, that spark usually dims. This is why the Lord tells us in Matthew 18:3 that if you become like a child you will enter the kingdom of heaven. This scripture is referring to faith.

If we're always asking for signs, do we really have faith?

There are times in my life where I've asked for signs about particular things I've had questions about. But if I received all the signs that I asked for in the way I wanted God to answer those questions, would I really have faith? There are times when the Lord provided those signs, but many when He didn't. Trusting Him is more important than an answer I may want to know in the moment, but I don't need to know. When Jesus was led into the wilderness to be tempted by the devil, Satan said, ""If You are the Son of God," "throw Yourself down. For it is written: 'He will command His angels concerning You, and they will lift You up in their hands, so that You will not strike Your foot against a stone.'" Jesus replied, "It is also written: Do not put the Lord your God to the test."

CHAPTER 8

Healing

Healing is oftentimes a very spiritual process. Healing takes time and it takes work. Can you fully heal from abuse, neglect, rejection, or seemingly other 'unforgivable' actions? Well, with God, all things are possible. Matthew 19:26 NIV: "With man this is impossible, but with God all things are possible". And Philippians 4:13 says, "I can do all things through Christ who strengthens me."

Seeking Justice

"But with everything I've gone through, how will I ever receive justice for the pain I have endured and the burden which came from it?" The truth is, we can't see the full justice we deserve on this earth. God judges all sins according to

His will. God does not call us to be the judge on anyone else's behalf. For He will hold us all accountable for our actions. Romans 12:19 states, "Beloved, never avenge yourselves, but leave it to the wrath of God; for it is written, 'Vengeance is mine, I will repay,' says the Lord".

Radical Healing

God can heal anyone. Let's break down the heavy topic, abuse. Abuse is a complicated concept to grasp when you hear that God can heal anyone. How does one heal from deep trauma? How can one live life with those deep roots sown into them? Abuse is a demonic attack, with the intent to hinder us, separate us from God, and diminish who God called us to be.

You may have received a crappy hand of cards; it's what you do with those cards that count.

Success begins when you lay everything down at the feet of Jesus. Over the winter of 2023-24, I traveled a decent amount. I extended my Christmas trip at home for a couple weeks because I just wanted to be away from California. I was questioning so many things. In a state of desperation, I finally laid it all at Jesus' feet. "I give it all to you, Jesus." It wasn't just because I said it but because I meant it in my heart. Jesus is after your heart. He knows your motives and He knows whether or not He is at the throne of your heart. When He's not at the throne of your heart, you're not winning. It's unfortunate that I've often reached my breaking point before I let Jesus take the throne of my life. It's so easy to idolize worldly achievements, items, animals, or even people before God.

Once I laid it all down, my life started to shift. In March of 2024, my best friend, Maddie, was getting married and asked me to be in the wedding. I sacrificed what I thought would have been a great opportunity to attend her wedding. But this was a once and a lifetime event and I couldn't not show up for my best friend's big day. There was just something about that trip back to Virginia - I knew in my heart that God was going to move me out of SoCal and reveal to me where that would be on this trip. A gym owner I met only a handful of times, reached out to me while I was in Virginia. He asked how I was doing and I gave him the honest rundown - nothing was going well. I was at the point of having mental breakdowns every single day and I was trying to get out of that state as much as possible. He had brought up the name of a training camp that he recommended to me a couple months back. I told him that I looked into it but couldn't afford the high price of their coaching. He said, "I want to reward you for taking the leap of faith and moving out there to chase your dreams. I'll pay for it for a year." Kind, genuine people exist in this world and God truly blessed me through that person.

Renewing of the mind
    Ephesians 4:23-24 ESV:

> "and to be renewed in the spirit of your minds, and to put on the new self, which is created after God's likeness in true righteousness and holiness."

It's God's will and desire for us to walk in full freedom.

When I lived in California, I spent the whole year in a toxic environment that ended up taking a rough toll on my mental health. When I moved to Georgia, I moved to what was a good environment and finally the only healthy gym environment I had ever been a part of. I didn't know what to do with myself but knew I needed to heal. God healed me throughout the past year, breaking off piece by piece of every burden over time.

CHAPTER 9

How Do You Hear God's Voice?

HEARING GOD SPEAK COMES in many different forms. Although there are many different ways that people hear the Lord's voice, here are some of the most common ways: thoughts, dreams, visions, pictures in their head, signs, gut feelings (which is even a gift of discernment) or an audible voice.

I have heard the Lord in all of these ways, however, the most frequent of these for me are through my thoughts. God is often teaching me something powerful through a thought that pops up out of nowhere. Sometimes He'll keep speaking through that one thought and I'm basically listening to a whole sermon in my head. I know they're not my thoughts because it's something so powerful and profound, I know I did not come up with it on my own.

How do I discern if I'm hearing my own thoughts, an attack from the enemy, or the Holy Spirit speaking to me? I once heard a very powerful quote: "If it's from God, it comes with peace and confirmation. If it's from the enemy, it comes with questions and confusion." I've found that every time I've come to make an important decision in life, and I chose the option I didn't have peace over, I always regretted it. And every time I've chosen the option that I had peace and no questions or confusion over, God truly blessed it.

It's important to pay close attention to your thoughts because ultimately, they will shape the reality of your life. *"Thoughts become words, words become actions, actions become habits, habits become character, character becomes destiny."* -- *Lao-Tze.*

The devil knows your strengths. He knows how the Lord speaks to you. I've been wondering why I get attacked so much in my thoughts. I've wondered why I've struggled with a lot of self-doubt throughout my life and sometimes it's not even relevant to me. I'll be working on a specific lift at the gym which is a strength of mine. Then all of the sudden, doubt just enters me and I keep failing at weights that I know I can hit. Why does this happen? God recently gave me a revelation about this. The reason I've been attacked so much through thoughts is due to the fact that it's counter to my strengths. God has given me a strong gift of faith. What's the definition of faith? Complete trust or confidence. It's having complete trust in God. So if the devil knows I have that gift, of course he will target me with a lack of self esteem and try to derail my trust in God. The enemy's number one goal is to separate us from God. So if you're facing struggles in an area of your life, if you've had a common theme of getting attacked in a specific way, take some time to dive deep into your gifts and the calling on your life. Ask God to reveal the reason you have struggled with those things. The next step is to work on patching up any holes in your life so that you don't leave an open door for the enemy. It's important to carry the full Armor of God so that you're prepared to shoot down any arrow that the devil throws at you.

Ephesians 6:10-18 NIV

> *10 Finally, be strong in the Lord and in his mighty power. 11 Put on the full armor of God, so that you can take your stand against the devil's schemes. 12 For our struggle is not*

against flesh and blood, but against the rulers, against the authorities, against the powers of this dark world and against the spiritual forces of evil in the heavenly realms. 13 Therefore put on the full armor of God, so that when the day of evil comes, you may be able to stand your ground, and after you have done everything, to stand. 14 Stand firm then, with the belt of truth buckled around your waist, with the breastplate of righteousness in place, 15 and with your feet fitted with the readiness that comes from the gospel of peace. 16 In addition to all this, take up the shield of faith, with which you can extinguish all the flaming arrows of the evil one. 17 Take the helmet of salvation and the sword of the Spirit, which is the word of God.

18 And pray in the Spirit on all occasions with all kinds of prayers and requests. With this in mind, be alert and always keep on praying for all the Lord's people.

The Lord has put it on my heart to work on tightening the belt of truth in my life. What does this look like? Having confidence in God's truth about my life so that the enemy can have no open door. This looks like: writing down God's promises and meditating on them. Standing up for myself with love for the other person. Valuing truth above feelings/emotions, rebuking (even out loud) any negative thought that enters my mind. Here's a prayer I learned a few years ago that has been helpful: "Lord, if there are any thoughts in my mind that do not come from the Father, the Son, or the Holy Spirit, please remove them in Jesus' name."

CHAPTER 10

Foundation of Truth

Don't give the devil the time of day.
Ephesians 4:21-27 NIV

WHEN YOU HEARD ABOUT Christ and were taught in him in accordance with the truth that is in Jesus. You were taught, with regard to your former way of life, to put off your old self, which is being corrupted by its deceitful desires; to be made new in the attitude of your minds; and to put on the new self, created to be like God in true righteousness and holiness. Therefore each of you must put off falsehood and speak truthfully to your neighbor, for we are all members of one body. "In your anger do not sin": Do not let the sun go down while you are still angry, and do not give the devil a foothold.

The devil will do anything he can to lead you off the path that God has set before you. He brings questions and confusion. God brings peace and understanding. Remember that anytime you're seeking discernment on a decision or in a situation.

God calls us to live above approach by putting on the full armor of God every day so that we don't leave any doors open for the enemy to creep in and have a foothold anywhere in our lives.

There are times to put a foot down and there are times to ignore attacks. Don't give Satan the time of day he's asking for. He wants to corrupt your life. It's important to learn how and when to fight back and call out his schemes and when to ignore the darts he's throwing at you. You can't give him any power over you. God has equipped you with the power to withstand any evil scheme.

Philippians 4:13 NIV I can do all this through him who gives me strength

Truth overrides emotions.

God calls us to stand up for what is right. And to stand up for what is right sometimes means standing up for yourself. As a Christian and as someone who has always been very intentful with words because of the way I've been abused by them, I have struggled to find proper boundaries.

1. Your words matter. The power of the tongue holds life or death. Are you speaking truth over your life or curses? Something even as simple as "I'm not good at"...*fill in the blank* is speaking a word curse over your life. What you say matters. The more negative you speak, the more your life is going to reflect those things. The more positive words you speak, your life will start to reflect it.

2. Be aware of what you're allowing in through your decisions. Pay attention to the music that you listen to. Is it uplifting or is it downgrading to your morals? We have to be aware of what we let through all gates: ear gates, eye gates... etc. If the Lord is convicting you about something, don't ignore it. The more that I spend time with the Lord, the more that He will convict me of worldly things I've allowed into myself, particularly music or television.

Romans 12:12:

> Therefore, I urge you, brothers and sisters, in view of God's mercy, to offer your bodies as a living sacrifice, holy and pleasing to

> God—this is your true and proper worship. Do not conform to the pattern of this world, but be transformed by the renewing of your mind. Then you will be able to test and approve what God's will is— his good, pleasing and perfect will.

Ask the Lord if there are any areas in your life where you have left a hole for the enemy to creep in. If the Lord reveals anything to you, it could be an immediate thought that comes to mind or through another way the Lord speaks to you, the next step is to bring it to the Lord in repentance. Ask the Lord for strength to not be deceived and wisdom to discern any traps from the enemy.

You need to have enough self respect to tell the truth if it means helping yourself or the other person. This does not mean just pointing out somebody's flaws just to prove you're right. It needs to be done with the right heart posture.

The Bible says to love others but we may often forget what love really means. Love is not easy. Love is sacrificial. True love stems from a sacrifice - the sacrifice of Jesus.

If someone doesn't receive constructive feedback with an open mindset then that's a reflection on their own immaturity.

I've had a distorted concept of what love really was. We live in a coddle culture where people are afraid to receive backlash for speaking out or are afraid to speak the truth because they don't want to hurt anyone's feelings. Love produces truth but it also comes with a pure heart - a non-religious spirit. A religious spirit is a sign of an immature believer.

If confronting someone, check yourself first. Make sure you're approaching with a pure heart and no anger. If you're all worked up, you're probably going to end up saying something that you'll regret. Never let pride (wanting to be liked) prevent you from speaking the truth. The truth is what sets people free. As Christian's, we're called to shed light on the truth of the Gospel, even if that means being persecuted for it.

Matthew 5:10-12 NIV:

> "Blessed are you when people insult you, persecute you and falsely say all kinds of evil against you because of me. Rejoice and be glad, because great is your reward in heaven, for in the same way they persecuted the prophets who were before you.

CHAPTER 11

Stomping on the Devil's Neck:

WHEN YOU ARE WALKING out your calling from the Lord, you will face spiritual warfare.

I've struggled immensely with dyslexia throughout my life. I've always had a difficult time with basic comprehension. I remember how difficult it was to learn the alphabet. After practicing multiplication tables every day, I still couldn't memorize most of them, even throughout high school. I'd spend 6+ hours on open book tests and end up with a C because I just couldn't transfer the information off the paper and into my brain. I was always known as the kid who smiled but hardly understood basic conversations. As a kid

I always got talked over when asked a question due to the awkward amount of time it took for me to comprehend the question being asked. I've always been misunderstood and it still occurs to this day. I thought I'd never be able to read a book and understand the plot of the story. That was until I was 13 and had learned how cane sugar can greatly hinder a dyslexic brain. After going off of it, my comprehension greatly improved. I still have difficulty with comprehension but I've learned how to manage it to the best of my abilities. Disabilities are not from the Lord. We live in an imperfect world and that was never God's intention but He gave us free will and that's where sin came into the world, bringing sickness and many other terrible things. But as much as I've suffered with a learning disability, God has blessed me with many wonderful things. I have received a blessing from my learning disability and that's grit. I've only ever had two options: work as hard as I can for something or give up and don't learn anything at all. From a young age I had to fight hard in order to learn anything. I've learned to push past what feels impossible in the moment and that gift has gotten me far in many different areas of life. In a workout, I know how to reach my threshold of what feels impossible in the moment and push through that painful barrier.

The devil tried to curse me with dyslexia but I utilized it for grit and here I am writing a book. The devil tried to curse me with asthma but I chose to follow the career God called me to in CrossFit anyway and got delivered from it. The devil tried to make me believe that my life wasn't worth living but God reminded me that He saved me for a reason when I was four and I have a big calling on my life. The devil tried to take my life multiple times by near death accidents but God had His hand of protection around me. The devil tried to make me quit the sport God called me into but God always provided. The devil tried to break my trust in God by throwing backstabbing people into my life but God has never let me down. The devil tried to attach dangerous false identities onto me but God always showed me who I truly am.

The devil's goal is to make you give up on your calling. That's why it's important to put on the armor of God, surround yourself with uplifting people, and stay rooted in faith. These are all essential for fighting off schemes of the enemy.

Distinguishing spiritual warfare versus God closing a door:
As I mentioned earlier, the toughest year of my life was 2023 - 2024 when I moved out to Southern California. Four months in when

nothing was going well, I became very confused. I knew that the Lord had called me out of my hometown and I believed that San Diego is where He called me to. And it was for a short time. I had never been treated so poorly and never felt so alone. One night when I had come off of my valet shift, I was driving home listening to a worship playlist. A new song with a slower start had come on and I almost skipped it until I heard "Just listen." The song is called "Lost in your Love" by Brandon Lake. It was the first time I had ever heard it and it truly made me emotional. The chorus goes, "I just want to be close to your heart. This is where my healing finds its start. Here is where I find my peace, where my soul is finally free." It was as if God was telling me in that moment, "Just stay close to my heart and everything will be okay." I spent so many nights listening to that song along with many other worship songs, crying out to God. My chapter in California was brutal but it truly grew me closer to the Lord where I learned to lean on Him and trust Him more than anybody. I was still waiting for an answer as to why I was there. I lost most of my joy and peace. But God restored it once He opened up the door for me to move to Georgia. A few days after I moved into my apartment in Georgia, I sat on the couch in the mostly empty apartment and just broke down in tears. It suddenly hit me how difficult the last year was and how much of a toll it had taken on me. I finally felt peace since I moved out of California. Then I heard God say, "I brought you out there to break the generational curse of rejection off of your life." Everything just made sense at that moment. After a year of intense torment and rejection, I fought hard and I leaned on the Lord. He broke off chains that had been weighing me down my whole life. You have got to walk through the fire in order to overcome it.

So was I facing warfare or was God closing a door? It was both in this situation. If you don't have peace or joy, it is not from the Lord. The enemy brings questions and confusion. God gives peace and confirmation. The enemy tried to destroy me through a year of torment and rejection. God let me move there to make me stronger and pulled me out of it when it was time.

It reminds me of the story of Job in the Bible. Job was a truly blessed man who had a fruitful family, livestock, and servants. Job loved the Lord with all his heart. The Bible states that he was the greatest man among all the people of the East. Satan himself came to the Lord and asked permission to curse Job. God gave Satan permission as long as Satan didn't lay a finger on Job himself. Satan tormented Job and took away everything he had: his family, his livestock, his house, every blessing that Job had. But Job, in all his sorrows, kept praising the Lord. Job looked past his current circumstances and focused on what's eternal. Job endured immense suffering but remained a faithful servant of the Lord. God allowed Job to be tested in every way. After all of the torment that Job faced, the Lord said that He blessed the latter part of Job's life more than the beginning. The Lord rewards those who remain faithful in heaven. Don't allow your circumstances to dictate your level of faith. Be strong where most others give up because your reward is not temporary but eternal.

Don't give any power over to the enemy.

Satan is the master at twisting the truth. He will take what you know is true and put question marks behind it. This has been the devil's tactic for separating people from God since the beginning of time. In the Garden of Eden, the serpent (Satan) manipulated Eve into sin by questioning what God told her.

> " Now the serpent was more crafty than any of the wild animals the Lord God had made. He said to the woman, "Did God really say, 'You must not eat from any tree in the garden'?" The woman said to the

serpent, "We may eat fruit from the trees in the garden, but God did say, 'You must not eat fruit from the tree that is in the middle of the garden, and you must not touch it, or you will die.'" "You will not certainly die," the serpent said to the woman. "For God knows that when you eat from it your eyes will be opened, and you will be like God, knowing good and evil."

I encourage you to read all of Genesis chapter 3. Pay attention to the wording Satan uses when he deceived Eve. He starts off by questioning what God said. Then he explains that eating the fruit will give her power. This is how the devil operates in his attempt to pull people away from Christ. Questioning and twisting the truth and offering some sort of "power" that will always lead to pain and destruction.

If you don't have a solid understanding of what God's word says and who He says you are, you're a vulnerable target for the enemy. I've spent most of my life as a Christian and I've struggled for most of it, knowing the truth about who I truly am. The enemy has had a foothold in my life in the past due to my vulnerability in not knowing my worth. As a victim of psychological abuse, it can unfortunately lead to the enemy knocking at your door in those vulnerable areas where you have been scarred. Truthfully, it's taken me a lifetime to put my foot down. I know that I'm worthy of love, worthy of success, worthy of freedom, worthy of joy, worthy to stand up for myself, worthy of a beautiful fulfilling life, all because of Jesus.

CHAPTER 12

The Power We Hold as Believers

THE LORD PROMISES HIS believers authority over the devil. Demons tremble at the mention of Jesus's name. When you confess Jesus as your Lord and Savior and give your life over to Him, the Holy Spirit lives inside of you. Luke 10:19 - NIV states: *I have given you authority to trample on snakes and scorpions and to overcome all the power of the enemy; nothing will harm you."* The devil can plot, bark, and throw boulders at you, but has no authority or power over you. It's very important to understand this as a believer. It's not through our own strength we can cast out demons but through the power of Jesus we have authority to do so by the Holy Spirit dwelling in us.

When I am having doubts that I know are not from the Lord, I often pray that the Lord will remove them. You have authority to take control over your thoughts. You have authority, through Jesus's name, to rebuke the devil and shut down the schemes he set up to throw you off your track. Something I wish I knew sooner in life is the power that I have through Jesus to not receive word curses over my life. When someone speaks a negative word over you, don't accept it. Because if you do, it can become an attachment onto your life. When you're accepting a word curse spoken over you, you're coming into agreement with the enemy's plan. They can be broken off, but it's best to nip it in the bud and never come into agreement with a word curse in the first place.

It makes me mad anytime I hear someone say that depression or an eating disorder can never truly go away. I'm here to testify that is a lie from the pit of hell and exactly what Satan wants people to come into agreement with. I faced disordered eating and God delivered me from it. I faced severe depression and God healed it. I don't struggle with either of these any more. The devil can tempt, but you have ultimate authority over that temptation and can rebuke it in Jesus's name.

One of the hardest things to wrap my head around in regards to my authority through Jesus has been rebuking sickness. Sickness does not come from the Lord. It came into the world when sin entered through Adam and Eve in the Garden of Eden. When Jesus died on the cross for our sins, He defeated all darkness, all sin and that includes sickness. Although there are many diseases that God doesn't heal, even through prayer, there's always a reason for it. But we do have authority to rebuke anything that is not of the Lord. We are given power through Jesus to rebuke sickness off of our lives. It's important not only to rebuke those things out loud but also have faith that God has all power and can heal anything or anyone.

Your words hold so much power. This is why it's important to pay attention to the words that come out of your mouth. They can be uplifting to your life or destructive to it. The other day, I started to feel sick. I had been exposed to many sick people throughout the week. My ears had so much pressure and I started to feel something in my throat. I was standing in my kitchen, about to sneeze, then I felt a nudge in my spirit to rebuke it. Why accept sickness into my life when Jesus already defeated it for me? I rebuked it in Jesus's name and in that moment I said, "I don't accept sickness into my life." Suddenly I didn't need to sneeze, my ears popped and all the pressure left at once and the tickle in my throat was gone.

You see, the devil consistently taunts people with bait by bringing inconveniences onto their lives, leaving them in a vulnerable state. Unfortunately, most people take the bait, which is when we accept defeat, (this was exactly his plan) opening the door for him to sink his teeth into your life, operating in oppressing you in that area. At this point, it's not too late to get out of, as Jesus can deliver us from anything. But it is going to take a lot of work.

No matter how much spiritual warfare you face, no matter how many things go wrong throughout your day, do not accept defeat. Do not fall back into sinful habits because that's what the devil wants you to do. Be careful with your words and do not come into agreement with any thoughts, words, or circumstances that are not of the Lord.

Conquering fear/doubts

There have been times throughout my life where I questioned if God was real for a moment. But then I remembered that moment where He brought me from death to life while I was all by myself in that mini van at four years old and that He told me I had a strong calling on my life.

I remember how different my life is now in comparison to how it was before I had a true relationship with the Lord and how He completely delivered me from severe depression, suicidal thoughts, OCD, anxiety, asthma, and an eating disorder.

I remember the time I was being prayed over for deliverance and God lifted off the generational curse of rejection from my life after walking through a severe season of it and facing it my whole life.

I remember how confused I was all the time when I didn't know if I wanted a relationship with God over the world.

I remember how God answered numerous prayers immediately and the ones He answered over time were well worth the wait.

I remember how miserable I was before I truly knew the Lord. How before Him, I lived in constant fear over the future of my life. I didn't live in peace before Him.

I still don't know the entire trajectory of my life but I'm completely at peace with that.

And if you ask me, "What if you're wrong?" I would say that I would rather submit everything I have and live my life knowing and feeling loved, valued, and at peace than take the risk of losing it again and not entering the kingdom of heaven.

Mathew 16:25 NCV For whoever wishes to save his life will lose it, but **whoever loses his life for my sake will find it.**

CHAPTER 13

Remove What's Hindering You

For every door the Lord closes, another door opens.

I rode horses competitively for nearly my whole life until I turned nineteen. When Sahara passed away, I had no idea it was going to take such a significant emotional toll as it did. It felt as if there was a hole in my heart. Something was missing in my life and I no longer felt complete. This was before I learned that I had a soul tie with her. For the first time, I realized that I depended on her for emotional health. Spending time with her and taking care of her was my coping mechanism. I replaced her with any friendships because she could never say anything to hurt me the way many people have in my life. When God is elevating you, He will remove what's hindering you to push the needle forward in your relationship with Him. For the first time, I learned that I didn't know how to cope with my emotions in a healthy way. Leaning on God for my emotional health hasn't been my first instinct. But by removing Sahara from my life, I have become a much healthier person. I finally learned the importance of healthy relationships. Using anything other than the Lord as a coping mechanism is like placing a bandaid over a deep wound that keeps reopening. It's a temporary fix but never a solution to the real, deep rooted issue.

My secondary coping mechanism to horses has been music. When I was feeling down, I would listen to music that reflected my emotions to help myself cope with a situation. But again, it's a bandaid placed over a deep, open wound that needs to get to the root of the issue. No matter how anxious or sad I feel, whenever I choose to play worship music, I instantly feel as if a weight has been lifted off of me. There's something about taking your eyes off of your own problems and fixing them on the Lord that never fails to lift up your spirit. God wants us to put Him as our first resort in every situation.

As believers, it can be easy to fall into a pattern of only giving the Lord our attention in specific situations. As for me, I've had the tendency to draw closest to the Lord when I'm in my darkest moments. How gracious is the Lord to love us and always provide even when we only give a little (or none) of our hearts.

But the more you fix your eyes on the Lord in all situations, the more fruitful and beautiful your relationship with Him will be. The Lord is jealous over your heart. He wants all of it. Think about your relationship with the Lord. Is it mostly one-sided or are you giving Him your whole heart?

Is there anything blocking you from walking into the fullness of God's plan for your life?

Grace is required to live freely. Sometimes we blame the devil for a hindrance that's really our own. Don't hinder your life by expecting too much from yourself. It's easy to set a goal. It's difficult to put it into action and succeed at it. I have a type A personality. I often place unrealistic expectations on myself then feel like a failure if I don't succeed at them. It's human nature to expect much from ourselves then self-sabotage when things go south. I've had to learn to give myself grace. I had to learn how to let go of my own plan when it was necessary. This is an extremely valuable lesson to learn in your walk with the Lord. You have to let go of your plan for your life and let Jesus take the reins.

It's better to admit you walked through the wrong door than to spend your life in the wrong room.

Is your environment hindering you or helping you progress?

When you're living in a toxic environment, it can have a hindering effect on your body, mind, and soul. But sometimes God allows us to suffer in those environments to serve a greater purpose in our lives or the lives of others. Contrary to popular belief, the devil is not to blame for everything. Even through the seasons where I have endured challenging atmospheres, those ultimately launched me into adulthood, helping me navigate manipulative people and strong setbacks in life whenever they pop up. So I am grateful to have learned from those experiences but excited to have that weight lifted off my shoulders so that I can excel in a positive environment and season moving forward.

Is your friend circle hindering you?

Take a moment to name your 5 closest friends. Now what are their top attributes? Do any of them gossip frequently? Do they pressure you into things that go against your convictions? Are they adding or subtracting from your life?

Friendships are blessings from God. Maybe you're not sure if a particular friend was sent from God or orchestrated from the enemy to lead you down the wrong path. I have wondered this about a few people in my life and have asked God for clarity. If you're not receiving clarity but this person has attributes that go against your convictions, take that as your sign to set boundaries. Sometimes we're asking God to remove something from our lives if it's hindering us but we can't always expect people to magically disappear from our lives. Sometimes we need to take initiative to draw boundaries. Even Jesus drew boundaries.

CHAPTER 14

Change your Perspective

Great success requires a strong mindset. You have more control over your mental state than you may think you do. I remember when I felt God calling me to pursue CrossFit but I felt stuck - like I wasn't moving forward very far. There was a gentleman at my gym I was having a conversation with about mental toughness. I said, "I feel like I've been holding back and not pushing the way I know I'm capable of in my workouts." "I agree," he said. Then he took a piece of paper and wrote this quote, 'What I had I gave, what I kept is lost forever.' Let that sink in. He said, "This is the day that it comes to a stop. You're going to push hard through this workout." That day launched me into a career where I have surpassed my past self in a crazy number of ways. I still have that piece of paper.

The next week, the same person told me about a big CrossFit licensed competition called The Pit Teen Throwdown in Three Rivers, Michigan. I trained three times a day, dialed in my nutrition, and actually lost 15lbs within that first month. Perhaps it was a little too intense for the first month, but I wasn't holding anything back. I nearly podiumed in a large division and it just set a spark in me - "This is what I want to do with my life," I thought to myself during an event. I've learned so many lessons since then. Like, don't come out with a risky strategy unless you truly know yourself as an athlete. And yeah, I got lost in the woods in the first event. It was only a few months after I was given that inspirational piece of paper that I would be moving across the country to follow my dream and train fulltime.

Through the setbacks I faced while pursuing this dream, and any call the Lord has put on my life, I've learned that you have to take control over your past trauma. It's incredibly difficult to not let it hinder you in some capacity. But that's where mental toughness comes in. You have to reframe trauma. As previously mentioned, "And we know that in all things God works for the good of those who love him, who have been called according to his purpose." - Romans 8:28 NIV. The Lord utilizes what the enemy meant for evil and turns it to good. Trauma makes you stronger. Without it, I wouldn't know my callings in life. It has shaped who I am. It has given me grace for others who are in pain or who feel misunderstood. Learning to find ways you can be grateful for it is going to remove that hindrance it has over you. You control whether or not it has an impact on your life. I'm not saying it justifies abuse but it is how you take control and ownership. It is how you move forward so that you can succeed in life with nothing holding you back. God has called you to live a life full of freedom and joy, and fulfillment. Being grateful for the positive ways that challenges have changed your life is the opposite of what the enemy wants and that's how you find peace.

One day I went out for a long run in the cold and kept thinking about how much I didn't want to do it and wanted to just settle back my pace. Then I remembered, "I don't have to do this - I GET to do this." I flipped my mindset and ended up getting a huge PR on that run. Your mental state affects your performance immensely.

Through the journey of following your dreams, you will face many challenges or (seemingly) setbacks. As cliche as it sounds, it's not so much about the end goal. It's about what happens on the journey to it. It's how God refines you. It's about how you learn to face conflict. It's about failing and learning from your failures which are really just going to launch you forward. How you perceive mistakes is going to have a major impact on the level of success you are going to reach.

How do I know if my dream is from God?

I remember when I was about eleven years old, I wanted to pursue horseback riding professionally. It started with a subtle desire because I wanted to have a successful riding career as a form of identity. Just the sound of that sentence strikes a big red flag to my ears now. I prayed that God would give me the desire to pursue it - God allowed me to have that desire and it grew very strong. God showed me sign after sign telling me to not pursue this sport but I kept ignoring every one of them. At that age, I learned that I was allergic to horses. My mom and I spent a year and six months looking for a pony that suited me. I lost count after 52 I tried out. There were so many times we almost purchased one, but the day before the purchase date, the animal got severely injured. There were so many closed doors. We then finally bought one which lasted for two months. We came to find out that this pony was drugged when we bought her and she was so dangerous, that after we sold her, the next owner put her down. I had many falls and the animal almost killed my mom. Eventually, my parents surprised me two weeks before my birthday with the sweetest pony in the world, Sketch. I was called to come down stairs on a random Saturday morning. I saw my parents standing on the porch, there was a trailer in the driveway with a banner on it. I opened the door, saw his sweet face, then went over to my mom, gave her a hug and cried. All of that heartache and waiting, I finally got a pony. I rode him three times that day.

When I outgrew my pony, Sketch, it was time to move up to a horse. Not long after looking, we found the horse of my dreams, Sahara. I loved her with all my heart. I had one year of getting used to her before everything started falling apart. The second year of owning her, every time we'd try to go to a horse show over the weekend, something prevented me from going such as: a wind storm knocked trees down on the road, rain came though, leaving the roads flooded, a family member ended up in the hospital... there was always something. My season was shot. The third year, she became lame all of the sudden. She randomly got a severe tendon injury in her leg and had to take a year off to recover. The fourth year, I felt the Lord asking me to switch over to CrossFit and leave the horse world behind. One night in January of 2021 at about 10:30, I went out to the barn to bring Sahara in for the night. Before walking out to her I stopped dead in my tracks and said, "If anything happens to this horse where she has to be put down, I'm moving on from this sport." A minute later, I found her in the field barely able to put one hoof in front of the other. She had a freak accident and bowed a tendon so badly, there was no coming back from it. Two days later she was put out of her misery.

God told me over and over again that pursuing that sport wasn't His plan for my life. I wondered how I could possibly leave a sport I worked for my entire life. How will I ever be able to catch up in another sport? But God's plan was way better than mine. When I truly started a relationship with God and not a check list, He placed new, healthy dreams in my heart that line up with His will for my life. Dreams are from the Lord. When we're not truly walking with Him, that's when we can be deceived by the devil, falling into his will for our lives which leads to destruction. It was when I said, "Here's my life Lord, it's all yours," that's when God placed those dreams on my heart that are His will for my life and has led me to a place of freedom and fulfillment.

CHAPTER 15

Avoid Toxic Empathy

I'M NATURALLY A VERY empathetic person. So I've had to learn the importance of setting boundaries the hard way. I see myself in someone else's shoes and feel their emotions deeply. However, it's not my place to feel the emotions of another person, even though there is value in having empathy for others, you can't allow it to drag yourself down.

It's not easy for me to admit that I have spent most of my life as a people pleaser. That is however, a statement that I now refuse to come into agreement with. It ultimately comes down to caring too much about what other people think. As

I've been in the process of renewing my mind-set towards other's opinions about my life, I've realized two important things to keep myself in check. 1: You relieve so much stress off of your life when you stop holding yourself hostage to others' potential opinions. 2. You'll feel much more at peace when you know you're stepping out of a door that held you back from God's plan for your life.

It takes repeated action and humility to step out of people pleasing. Stop caring so much about what the world thinks and fix your mind on what's above. If you've known that a situation you're in hasn't been where God wants you to be but you're afraid to exit for the sake of people who will treat you poorly or even take it to the level of abuse, diligently seek the Lord and ask for a peaceful way out.

It takes an awful lot of getting pushed down before you may realize that you're worth standing up for yourself. I feel like I've been given test after test to see if I'll take a stand for myself. From being bullied as a kid and adolescent, to employers abusing me, and many other people trying to take advantage of me, it gets to a point where you're sick of getting knocked down. You have a voice and you have free will to use it.

I've always been one to feel things deeply. That's why I hate when people tease me and I'm very cautious about the words I speak to people. I've spent most of my life not standing up for myself because I'm afraid of saying something to hurt someone the same way I have been hurt. I've spent too much of my life worrying about hurting someone by speaking the truth cause that's love isn't it? No. That's called toxic empathy. We live in a coddle culture where people are afraid to tell the truth because it might get them canceled. Now there's a time to be truthful when it matters and a time to keep quiet when it's necessary. It's important to have a heart posture of speaking to another person out of love, not out of a legalistic take because that's not love, and a condescending behavior is going to rub someone the wrong way. And if someone takes the truth you give them out of love in the wrong way, if they can't treat you like a friend for having a different point of view, that person probably doesn't need to be in your life.

CHAPTER 16

Never Give up on the Calling

MAYBE GOD IS PUTTING your calling on hold because He knows you're going to put your identity in it over Him.

I've known since the first year I started CrossFit, that God was calling me to it. He's given me gifts mentally and physically to excel in the sport. There has been a pattern repeated throughout my life: everything I have been called to, I've endured intense spiritual attacks. They come through narcissistic, backstabbing people, through physical attacks, emotional/mental attacks, or natural phenomenons. Something that I dealt with all the way until this point were asthma attacks. It's very difficult to excel in a sport that mostly revolves around lung capacity when your lungs easily start closing up in a workout. I've been in the sport for six years now. I've had many doubts but I never doubted that God would provide a way for what I know He called me into. It's so frustrating to pursue a dream that is currently physically impossible to achieve. Since I moved to Georgia, my asthma got so bad, I was having asthma attacks every week. There wasn't a single workout where I wasn't heavily hyperventilating and I had to nearly stop as I could feel my throat closing up. Inhalers did not help. And that confirmed to me that I was right about why I suffered from asthma. It was a spiritual attack to lead me off the path that God has set before me.

One Thursday night, I was at small group with many of the girls from the gym. At the end of study, we were praying over the women who had prayer requests. I felt the Lord put it on my heart to ask for prayer. So they laid hands on me and were praying and prophesying healing in my lungs. It was a day or two after that, I had done a tough variation of a qualifier workout where I had a brutal asthma attack each time I attempted it. Almost immediately into starting the workout, an asthma attack began. It was 6 rounds with a 2 minute rest after every two rounds. During the first set, I kept rebuking it under my breath. The devil can't get access to your thoughts but can hear your words so you need to rebuke attacks verbally. During the second set, I kept rebuking it again but it kept happening. Then by the third set, it finally stopped and I gained control over my lungs. I ended the workout shocked at what had just happened. I've never been able to gain control like that during an intense asthma attack. That day was the last time that I have had any asthma. It's been three months now, and God has fully set me free from it. I can run tough intervals for the first time in my life and not be limited by my lungs. I feel like I can breathe for the first time. I went from having asthma every day to being completely free from it and I give all the credit to Jesus.

Opinions Don't Define You

When you're not confident who you are, you are susceptible to believing many lies that people will speak over you. When you're taking your daily bread consistently, you are less susceptible to believing the lies of the enemy because you're rooting your mind in truth. God warns us about how cunning the devil is in his schemes, seeking to devour the children of God any chance he gets.

All for God's Glory

If the dream isn't slightly delusional, you're probably not dreaming big enough. God will provide what you need for whatever He has called you to do. If God has placed a calling on your heart, it's going to come to pass as long as you stick with it.

Stop being a surface level thinker and have faith.

Hebrews 11:1 CSB Now faith is the reality of what is hoped for, the proof of what is not seen.

When you have so much confidence in who God says you are, you don't care so much about what other people think. You're not meant to fit in with the world - you're meant to stand out. If people notice that you're not like the rest of the world, you're probably on the right track.

A Bible verse in your Instagram bio doesn't make you a Christian. You can discern that by the fruit you produce. The knowledge and the wisdom that you share doesn't make you a Christian. Going to church doesn't make you a Christian. Following Jesus and surrendering your life to Him is what it means to be a Christian. The Bible makes this very clear.

A relationship with God doesn't look perfect for anybody. But the more you seek Him, the more you will find Him. The devil will do anything to distract you and attack you. But Jesus tells us that if you have Him in your heart, you have power and authority through Him, to overcome any scheme of the enemy. 1 John 4:4 NIV: "You, dear children, are from God and have overcome them, because the one who is in you is greater than the one who is in the world."

For what makes you special, it's important to know that the devil will use your gifts against you if you don't have solid grounding in who you are and who God created you to be. One of the most common mislabeled gifts I've seen is the gift of discernment. It is often mislabeled as bipolar disorder or BPD (Bordering Personality Disorder). You will never feel understood unless you understand that this is a spiritual gift from God, with the purpose of giving you insight into the spiritual realm so that you knock down arrows from the enemy, have awareness of spiritual battles, identify what's true and what's not, and lift people up by words of encouragement.

I've met people who have seen demons and been attacked by them but they don't believe in God. It made me wonder how someone can experience so much darkness but not believe in the light. Here's the harsh reality of this situation. If someone has never seen the light, if they don't believe God is real but have experienced torment from demons, they're most likely possessed by them and may not know it. If you have accepted

Jesus into your heart, demons cannot enter you. You can't be possessed as a believer but you can be oppressed by them and in that case, you should seek deliverance from a fellow believer who knows how to properly walk you through it.

CHAPTER 17

Moving the Needle

WHEN YOU BELIEVE THAT everything works out for good, your life will significantly improve. When you believe with your whole heart that every tragedy, every "set back," every ounce of pain in your life can serve a purpose, you will never stop moving the needle forward in your life.

Genesis 50:20 NIV You intended to harm me, but God intended it for good to accomplish what is now being done, the saving of many lives.

Let me be clear, this does not mean to ignore the time to weep when it's time to weep or to mourn with those who are suffering. We're created to endure these times and express our natural emotions. However, we're not meant to stay there for long. We're not meant to live in bondage by our past. God created us to be victors, to rise up in the midst of everything the devil intended to tear us apart with.

Don't be complacent in expecting God's providence

A common thread in Christianity is the misconception of faith which can lead to complacency. The Bible tells us in James 2:17 that "Faith without works is dead." God has set your path before you, already mapped out. But if you are not working for what the Lord has put on your heart, and just wait around expecting everything to fall into your lap, you're missing the call.

Matthew 7:7-8 NIV "Ask and it will be given to you; seek and you will find; knock and the door will be opened to you. For everyone who asks receives; the one who seeks finds; and to the one who knocks, the door will be opened.

Patience in His Timing

Ecclesiastes 3:11NIV

> He has made everything beautiful
> in its time. He has also set eternity
> in the human heart; yet no one can
> fathom what God has done from
> beginning to end.

God will reveal the calling He has for your life - in His timing.

He works all things together for good

Life doesn't need to be overcomplicated. When you dedicate your life to the Lord, He will truly turn anything the enemy meant for evil into good. Think of your life as a puzzle. God sees the whole beautiful picture on the box, while you haven't yet seen it - only glimpses of some pieces but you're trying to figure it all out. Every season that God has placed you in, every job you've ever worked or ever will work, every close person in your life, they're all pieces of your puzzle. Without these lessons, without these people, without the set backs, without the victories, your puzzle would never complete. God has not placed darkness into your life, but allowed you to face it so that you may be whole and complete, having the revelation of God's calling on your life.